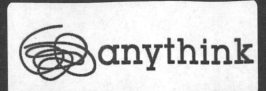

MIDNIGHT TEACHER
LILLY ANN GRANDERSON AND HER SECRET SCHOOL

BY JANET HALFMANN ☙ ILLUSTRATED BY LONDON LADD

Lee & Low Books Inc. • New York

This story is true to the known facts of Lilly Ann Granderson's life and the realities of society during the time she lived. However, in crafting this biography, the author included some imagined scenes, people, and thoughts. These parts of the story are dramatic extensions of historically documented events and interactions.

LEE & LOW BOOKS Inc., 95 Madison Avenue, New York, NY 10016
leeandlow.com
Book design by David and Susan Neuhaus/NeuStudio
Book production by The Kids at Our House
The text is set in Cochin
The illustrations are rendered in acrylic and colored pencil on illustration board

Manufactured in China by Jade Productions, December 2017
Printed on paper from responsible sources
10 9 8 7 6 5 4 3 2 1
First Edition

Library of Congress Cataloging-in-Publication Data
Names: Halfmann, Janet, author. | Ladd, London, illustrator.
Title: Midnight teacher : Lilly Ann Granderson and her secret school / by
Janet Halfmann; illustrated by London Ladd.
Description: New York : Lee & Low Books, 2018. | Includes bibliographical
references and quotation sources.
Identifiers: LCCN 2017010372 | ISBN 9781620141632 (hardback)
Subjects: LCSH: Granderson, Lilly Ann, 1821-1889. | African
Americans — Biography — Juvenile literature. | Educators — United
States — Biography — Juvenile literature. | African American
educators — Biography — Juvenile literature. | Women educators — United
States — Biography — Juvenile literature. | African
Americans — Education — Mississippi — History.
Classification: LCC LA2317.G628 H35 2018 | DDC 371.10092 [B] — dc23
LC record available at https://lccn.loc.gov/2017010372

For everyone who has somehow been touched
and inspired by Lilly Ann Granderson's great love
of learning and her teaching —J.H.

To all my art instructors. Thank you for your
encouragement and believing in me —L.L.

From a young age, Lilly Ann Eliza Cox believed the path to freedom was through education. Born into slavery around 1821 in Petersburg, Virginia, Lilly Ann was the youngest of four sisters. When she was around four years old, her mother died, and Lilly Ann was sold to a family in Kentucky.

Young Lilly Ann worked in the master's house. When the adults weren't watching, the master's children often played school with her. They even found an old ragged blue-back speller for Lilly Ann to use and keep.

While it was not illegal in Kentucky for enslaved people to learn to read and write, it was strongly discouraged. Lilly Ann knew to hide her blue-back speller in her pocket and practice her letters when no one was watching. She secretly traced words in the dirt of the garden and the spilled flour on the kitchen table as she worked. She was proud when she was finally able to write down her thoughts and read the Bible by herself.

Lilly Ann read everything she could get her hands on. Through newspapers lying about, she learned of places in the North where slavery had been abolished. She longed for freedom too.

As Lilly Ann's reading and writing skills improved, she wanted to share her knowledge with others. She found the perfect opportunity on Sundays when the master's family was away at church and visiting friends. Lilly Ann gathered other enslaved children and headed to the nearby woods. There, in a hidden spot, she taught them what she knew.

Lilly Ann formed a letter *A* with twigs, then helped the others make their own. She sang out the *A* sounds, and the new learners repeated after her. Her students traced the letters with their fingers to help them remember. As the group learned more letters, they formed words and then sentences. News of Lilly Ann's teaching spread, and more and more people of all ages joined her. Whenever her students mastered a new skill, Lilly Ann felt a burst of hope for a better future for them.

For many years Lilly Ann looked forward to teaching secretly every Sunday. Then her life was shattered overnight. Her master died, and his property was divided and auctioned off. Lilly Ann was sold down the Mississippi River to a plantation near Natchez, Mississippi.

Mississippi was not like Kentucky. In the "Lower South" cotton was king, and hundreds of thousands of enslaved people were forced to work in the fields from dawn until the sun went down.

For the first time Lilly Ann had to toil in the cotton fields. She was not used to the hard physical labor and blazing sun, and struggled to keep up with the others. Day after day the overseer whipped her. Lilly Ann thought she would "die from such cruel whippings."

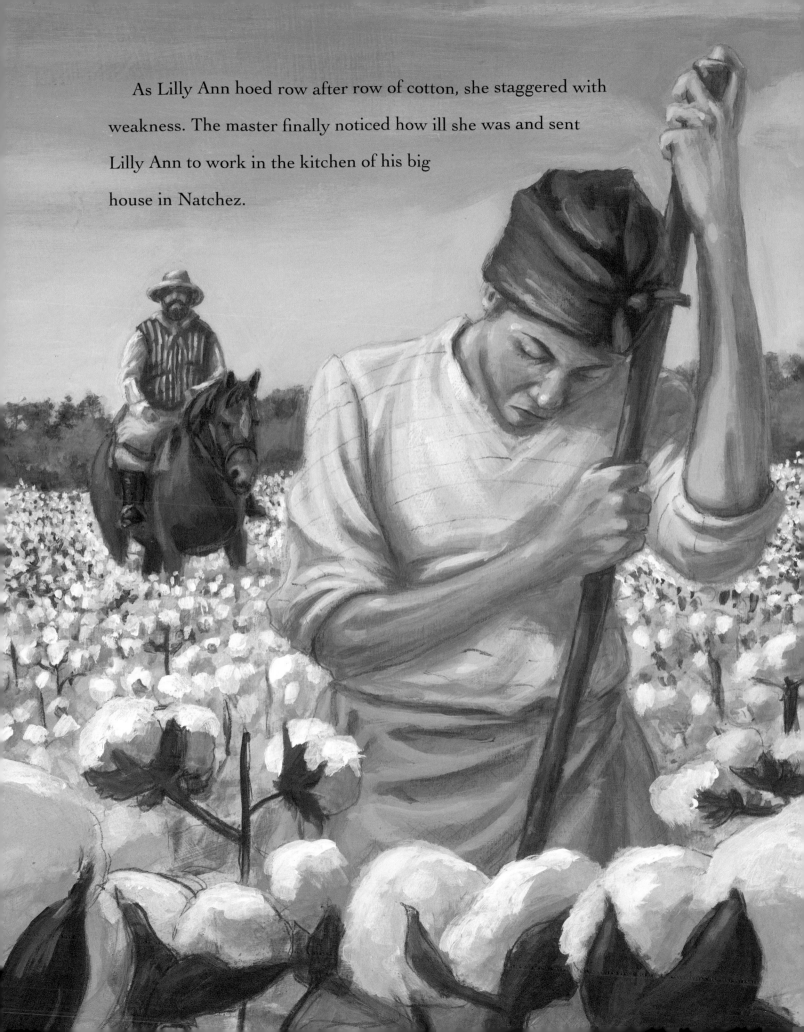

As Lilly Ann hoed row after row of cotton, she staggered with weakness. The master finally noticed how ill she was and sent Lilly Ann to work in the kitchen of his big house in Natchez.

Lilly Ann met a kind man named Oliver Granderson. After a few years, the couple had a son. While working long hours for her master, Lilly Ann wondered about her son's future. She realized she missed teaching and seeing her students' hopeful faces as they learned to read and write. She wanted to give others that hope again and decided to start another school.

This time, however, the risks were much higher. It was illegal in Mississippi for enslaved people to learn to read and write. Landowners feared that if the enslaved could read, they would discover that some northerners wanted slavery abolished. This might lead to rebellion against the owners. Many southern states required enslaved people to carry a pass from their master any time they traveled away from home. Knowing how to write would let them create their own passes, fool the authorities, and escape to freedom.

The punishment if Lilly Ann was found teaching would be thirty-nine lashes with a whip—for both her and her students. Despite the risks, Lilly Ann was determined to give her people the paths to freedom that education made possible.

For her new school Lilly Ann would need to find a place hidden from prying eyes. Luckily, she knew Natchez well from going to the market and running errands for her master. She found a secluded cabin off a back alley in town. Classes would have to be held in the middle of the night to avoid getting caught.

Word of Lilly Ann's midnight school spread quickly through the town's enslaved community. Details about the school were whispered to carriage drivers, and they in turn shared the news with others as they traveled around town.

After toiling for their masters all day, Lilly Ann's students slipped nervously into the town's shadowy night. Like alley cats, they crept through the darkness. They took twisty routes to keep from giving away their destination if they were ever followed.

Lilly Ann hated leaving Oliver and their young son every night, but she was willing to make the sacrifice to help others. She got to the school first to greet her new learners and ease their fears. Once the students arrived, they sealed the windows and door to avoid being discovered. Every noise in the night reminded them of the painful punishment they faced if they were found out.

No matter how tired everyone was from a long day's work, Lilly Ann's students—young and old—were eager to learn. They carefully studied the ragged spelling book that Lilly Ann had secretly brought from Kentucky. She helped her pupils sound out the letters and words, calming their jitters with her quiet voice and motherly face.

Crowded around their midnight teacher, the group took turns reading the Bible. Sometimes they brought books or newspapers taken from their owners' houses. Using sticks dipped in homemade ink, the new learners practiced writing their names on slates smoothed from pine.

One day a student had a surprise for Lilly Ann. Slowly, he wrote the word *FREEDOM*. The others hurried to copy the new word. Lilly Ann's eyes flooded with tears of joy.

Lilly Ann's belief that education was the key to a better future only grew stronger over the years. She took on twelve students at a time and taught them all she could. Then she started with another twelve.

Her students went on to share what they learned with their families, who beamed with pride that one of their own could read and write. Some students started secret schools of their own. Others used their new skills to write passes to escape to freedom in the North, just as Lilly Ann had hoped they would.

For seven years Lilly Ann and her students risked their safety and stayed up half the night practicing their lessons. Hundreds of enslaved people learned to read and write under their midnight teacher's patient but passionate guidance.

Then one dark, moonless night, a slave patrol noticed a tiny ray of light coming from the hidden cabin. The student guarding the door heard the patrollers' horses and alerted those inside to snuff out their lights and hide their books.

It was too late. The patrollers crashed through the door. Lilly Ann and her students froze, expecting to be punished right on the spot. The patrol leader ordered the school closed and told everyone to go straight home. He warned Lilly Ann and her students to expect thirty-nine lashes with a whip the next day.

The discovery of the school created a great deal of commotion among
Lilly Ann's master, the other slave owners, and local and state officials.
They debated what to do with Lilly Ann and her students.

Lilly Ann trembled with dread. Would they be whipped for wanting to
learn? Would she be separated from Oliver and her son? Despite all her
fears, Lilly Ann did not regret starting her school.

Finally, after weeks of waiting and worrying, an official came to speak to Lilly Ann's master. Lilly Ann held her breath, expecting the worst. To her surprise, the official told her master that Lilly Ann could teach, as authorities "found no law against a slave teaching a slave." Neither she nor her students would be punished.

Lilly Ann couldn't believe her ears. She took the good news as a direct answer to her prayers and was determined more than ever to educate her people. She reopened her school and started a Sabbath church school as well.

Lilly Ann was still teaching when a civil war began between the Northern and the Southern states. The two sides disagreed on whether slavery should be allowed in the nation's new territories. Because President Abraham Lincoln opposed the spread of slavery, the Southern states broke away from the United States to form the Confederate States of America. The Northern states remained the United States of America, or the Union.

In 1863, Union soldiers captured Natchez. They were surprised to find not only a school taught by Lilly Ann, but a great number of educated enslaved people in the town too. Union Army Chaplain Joseph Warren visited Lilly Ann's school and was very much impressed by it. He praised her as "a remarkable woman" who "taught many to read, at the risk of her life."

The Union takeover brought the freedom promised by the Emancipation Proclamation to Natchez. Lilly Ann and her family celebrated with a wedding. After being together for many years, on July 20, 1864, Lilly Ann and Oliver were legally married. It was a right that was previously denied to those enslaved.

Lilly Ann was also free to enjoy her love of learning any time she pleased. Sitting on the porch, she proudly read out loud to her family.

After the Civil War ended in 1865, newly freed people of all ages
longed for an education. Without the slave laws that forced them to study
in secret, they wanted their schools to be open and available the entire
year. Most teachers from the North, however, couldn't stand the steamy
heat and went home for the summer.

Lilly Ann shared her students' great enthusiasm for learning. During the summer of 1865, she and another formerly enslaved woman taught a class of 275 students. Lilly Ann's passion for education didn't stop there. She continued to teach and promote learning until late in her life.

Lilly Ann Granderson's inspiration lives on today through all the generations changed forever by her dedication to helping others gain freedom and improve their lives through education.

AFTERWORD

In historical records Lilly Ann Granderson is sometimes identified by the first name Lily, Lillie, or Lila; the last name Grandison; or the name Milla Granson. Her exact year of birth is unknown, although several historical documents

Union School, a public school in Natchez where Lilly Ann Granderson taught for many years after the Civil War.

Courtesy of Historic Natchez Foundation

support 1821, including her death notice, which states that she was sixty-eight when she died in 1889. There are few records regarding her family history and it is not known if any of Lilly Ann's family went with her when she was sold as a young child to an owner in Kentucky. During slavery, family members often were sold to different owners, tearing loved ones apart.

It is unclear why Lilly Ann and her students were not punished when her midnight school was discovered. Even though an official said "they found no law against a slave teaching a slave," the Mississippi Code of 1823 clearly banned the practice. Perhaps Lilly Ann's owner, who had the final authority over his "property,"

felt she would not turn others against slavery and therefore chose not to punish her. Also, in cities, laws against learning to read and write were not always as strictly enforced as in rural areas. Whatever the reason, Lilly Ann was overjoyed to be able to continue to teach and improve the lives of countless people.

As the Civil War came to an end in 1865, Lilly Ann knew she needed more knowledge to keep ahead of her students. She attended a church-sponsored school for newly freed women in the afternoon and taught in the morning. When a system of public schools began in Mississippi in 1870, she joined its staff and taught at Union School for many years.

In the late 1870s, Lilly Ann took on another educational challenge. The Baptist church wanted to create a seminary in Natchez to train black teachers and ministers, but to succeed, it needed wide community support. Lilly Ann led the effort, going from home to home, talking up the school, and encouraging young people to enroll. By the end of the first school year, in 1878, sixty students attended Natchez Seminary (now Jackson State University). Lilly Ann also served as a deaconess for Pine Street Baptist Church and a trustee of the Jacobs Benevolent Society.

Lilly Ann and Oliver Granderson had three children together. The couple proudly watched their own children attend school. Their son David, born around 1846, became a teacher and a minister after attending Oberlin College in Ohio. Their daughter Lilly Ann, born on February 25, 1862, headed up the first class of graduates from Natchez Seminary, the school her mother had championed. And like her mother, she dedicated her life to teaching and church work. Unfortunately, nothing is known about the couple's third child.

Lilly Ann Granderson died of tuberculosis on April 27, 1889, and was buried in Natchez City Cemetery. Today she and her midnight school are remembered during Civil War living-history events in Natchez.

In a visit to the Chicago home of Lilly Ann's great-granddaughter Clara Mae Bray and her great-great-grandson Agis Bray Jr. (both now deceased), they remarked to the author that education had been important in the family for as long as they could remember. The family's history spotlights the influence Lilly Ann had through many generations.

In 1901 Lilly Ann's granddaughter Jane Anna Granderson was one of the first two college graduates of Spelman Seminary (now Spelman College) in Atlanta, Georgia.

Lilly Ann's grandson Charles C. Diggs Sr., who moved to Detroit, Michigan, was a wealthy businessman and community activist, and became the first African American Democrat elected to the Michigan State Senate, in 1936.

Lilly Ann's great-grandson Charles C. Diggs Jr. was the first African American to represent Michigan in the United States Congress, serving from 1955 to 1980. He was a founder and the first chairman of the Congressional Black Caucus, a voice for African American issues.

We can only imagine the many achievements Lilly Ann's students and their families went on to accomplish because of their education—the everlasting legacy of a brave and dedicated teacher.

SELECTED REFERENCES

Adams Co., MS Genealogical and Historical Research. "Adams County Sexton Records." Compiled by Robert "Bob" Shumway. Accessed March 14, 2007. http://www.natchezbelle.org/adams-ind/sexton.htm.

Adams Co., MS Genealogical and Historical Research. "Natchez, Adams County, Mississippi, 1886 Census, 2nd Ward Inhabitants D–H." Compiled by Robert "Bob" Shumway. Accessed March 14, 2007. http://www.natchezbelle.org/adams-ind/2nd_d-h.htm.

Ancestry.com. "1870 United States Federal Census: D C Granderson." Accessed March 7, 2007.

Ancestry.com. "1880 United States Federal Census: Ann L. Granderson." Accessed March 7, 2007.

Ancestry.com. "Freedman's Bank Records, 1865–1874" for Lily Ann Granderson and D C Granderson. Accessed February 28, 2007 and March 8, 2007, respectively.

Bardwell, J. P. correspondence with M. E. Strieby. New Orleans, LA: American Missionary Association Archives, Amistad Research Center, 1865.

Behrend, Justin J. "Freedpeople's Democracy: African-American Politics and Community in the Postemancipation Natchez District." PhD diss., Northwestern University, 2006.

Code of Mississippi: Being an Analytical Compilation of the Public and General Statutes of the Territory and State, with Tabular References to the Local and Private Acts, from 1798–1848. Compiled by A. Hutchinson. Jackson, MS: Price and Fall, State Printers, 1848.

Dansby, B. Baldwin. *A Brief History of Jackson College.* Jackson, MS: Jackson College, 1953.

Davis, Ronald L. F. *The Black Experience in Natchez, 1720–1880.* Denver: US Department of the Interior, National Park Service, 1993.

Extracts from Reports of Superintendents of Freedmen. First Series. Compiled by Rev. Joseph Warren. Vicksburg, MS: Freedmen Press Print, 1864.

Family obituary of Lilly A. Granderson Diggs, 1937. Typed document provided to the author by the family.

FamilySearch.org. "Oliver Granderson: United States, Freedmen's Bureau Marriages, 1861–1872." Accessed May 18, 2011. https://familysearch.org/ark:/61903/1:1:F1XM-NTY.

Freedmen's Bulletin, The 1, no. 6 (1865): 101.

Haviland, Laura S. *A Woman's Life-Work: Labors and Experiences of Laura S. Haviland.* Cincinnati, OH: Walden & Stowe, 1882.

Natchez City Cemetery. Personal correspondence regarding Lilly Ann Granderson's death notice and burial, September 24, 2012 and April 12, 2017.

Span, Christopher M. *From Cotton Field to Schoolhouse: African American Education in Mississippi, 1862–1875.* Chapel Hill: The University of North Carolina Press, 2009.

Williams, Heather Andrea. *Self-Taught: African American Education in Slavery and Freedom.* Chapel Hill: The University of North Carolina Press, 2005.

Quotation Sources

p. 12: "die from such cruel whippings": Haviland, p. 300.

p. 28: "found no law against a slave teaching a slave": Haviland, p. 301.

Back cover and p. 30: "a remarkable woman" and "taught many to read, at the risk of her life": *Extracts from Reports of Superintendents of Freedmen*, p. 48.

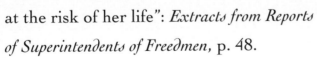

Acknowledgments

Special thanks to Justin J. Behrend, associate professor of history at SUNY Geneseo, for reviewing the story for historical accuracy, aiding with research sources, and answering questions, and to Edith Campbell, assistant librarian, Indiana State University, for reviewing and providing meaningful insight. Special thanks also to the descendants of Lilly Ann Granderson for their support and help in telling this story, especially great-granddaughter Clara Mae Bray and great-great-grandson Agis Bray Jr. (both now deceased), and Agis's wife, Irby. Thanks also to Ronald E. Butchart, distinguished research professor emeritus, Department of Educational Theory and Practice, University of Georgia, and to Christopher M. Span, associate professor, Department of Education Policy, Organization, and Leadership, University of Illinois at Urbana-Champaign, for assisting with research sources and answering questions. Also thanks to Christopher Harter of the Amistad Research Center, and many others for aiding with research. Much gratitude to Mimi Miller, executive director of the Historic Natchez Foundation, for guiding me in Lilly Ann Granderson's footsteps during my visit to Natchez, Mississippi, and for assisting with research and photos. A special thanks to my editor, Jessica Echeverria, and illustrator, London Ladd, for helping me bring Lilly Ann Granderson's story to life.